SNAPPING TURTLES

Bethany Baxter

PowerKiDS press
New York

Published in 2014 by The Rosen Publishing Group, Inc.
29 East 21st Street, New York, NY 10010

First Edition

Editor: Julia Quinlan
Book Design: Greg Tucker

Photo Credits: Cover tillsonburg/iStockphoto.com; pp. 4, 5 Ryan M. Bolton/Shutterstock.com; p. 6 Jason Patrick Ross/Shutterstock.com; p. 7 Bill Curtsinger/National Geographic/Getty Images; p. 8 Rex Lisman/Flickr/Getty Images; p. 9 Steve and Dave Maslowski/Photo Researchers/Getty Images; p. 10 swissmacky/Shutterstock.com; p. 11 Tony Campbell/Shutterstock.com; pp. 12–13 Larry Landolfi/Photo Researchers/Getty Images; p. 14 E R Degginger/Photo Researchers/Getty Images; p. 15 Debra Millet/Shutterstock.com; p. 16 Olgysha/Shutterstock.com; p. 17 George Grall/National Geographic/Getty Images; p. 18 Leonard Lee Rue III/Photo Researchers/Getty Images; p. 19 (top) mallardg500/Shutterstock.com; p. 19 (bottom) Matt Jeppson/Shutterstock.com; p. 20 Fotosearch/Getty Images; p. 21 Andrea J. Smith/Shutterstock.com; p. 22 Benjamin Simeneta/Shutterstock.com.

Library of Congress Cataloging-in-Publication Data

Baxter, Bethany.
 Snapping turtles / by Bethany Baxter. — 1st ed.
   p. cm. — (Awesome armored animals)
 Includes index.
 ISBN 978-1-4777-0795-1 (library binding) — ISBN 978-1-4777-0962-7 (pbk.) —
 ISBN 978-1-4777-0963-4 (6-pack)
 1. Snapping turtles—Juvenile literature. I. Title.
 QL666.C539B39 2014
 597.92'2—dc23
                              2012049561

Manufactured in the United States of America

CPSIA Compliance Information: Batch #S13PK6: For Further Information contact Rosen Publishing, New York, New York at 1-800-237-9932

Contents

Snapping turtles are **reptiles**. They are known for snapping, or trying to bite, at people or animals that come too close. Snapping turtles have very powerful jaws. A snapping turtle can easily bite off a person's finger! Snapping turtles also have natural armor to keep them safe from **predators**. They have hard upper shells with jagged back edges to protect their soft insides.

Alligator snapping turtles are closely related to common snapping turtles. They are bigger and live longer.

This snapping turtle is showing off its powerful jaws.

There are two species of snapping turtles. These are the common snapping turtle and the alligator snapping turtle. Snapping turtles are often called snappers. They are related to other turtles and tortoises, including sea turtles, pond turtles, and box turtles.

Watery Homes

Common snapping turtles can be found in parts of North America and northern South America. Their **range** stretches from southern Canada down to along the Gulf of Mexico. In the United States, they can be found from the Rocky Mountains to the Atlantic Ocean.

Snapping turtles spend some of their time outside of the water.

Snapping turtles are good swimmers. This turtle lives in Florida.

Snapping turtles live in many different aquatic, or watery, **habitats**. These include shallow freshwater marshes, creeks, swamps, bogs, pools, lakes, streams, and rivers. Snapping turtles can also live in brackish water, which is a mixture of freshwater and salt water. Snapping turtles like their aquatic habitats to have sandy or muddy bottoms. They do not like fast-moving water.

Snapping turtles have large heads and long necks. They have sharp jaws with rough edges for cutting food. The upper jaw is hook-shaped.

A snapping turtle's hard upper shell is called a carapace. Their carapaces grow to be about 8 to 14 inches (20 cm to 35.5 cm) long. They can be brown, green, or black. The back edge of the carapace is very jagged.

Common snapping turtles have webbed feet with long claws.

Snapping turtles' thick shells help keep them safe from predators.

The snapper's bottom shell is called a plastron. The plastron is small, which lets the turtle move easily.
Snapping turtles also have long tails covered in raised scales. Their tails can be as long as, or even longer than, their carapaces.

Snapping turtles spend most of their time in the water. They are nocturnal, or most active at night. During the day, they bury themselves in the sandy or muddy bottoms of their aquatic homes.

Snapping turtles need to bask in the Sun to keep their bodies from getting too cold. They generally do this by floating at the surface of the water. They may also leave the water to bask on the shore.

When they are on land, snapping turtles can be **aggressive**. They may attack people or animals that come too close. However, in the water, they quickly swim away when they become scared.

This snapping turtle is warming itself up by basking in the Sun.

Snapping Turtle Facts!

1. Snapping turtles can live in water that has become very **polluted**. Sometimes, snapping turtles are found in underground sewer systems in towns and cities.

2. Snapping turtles can go for two weeks without water. This lets them move across land from one body of water to another.

3. Common snapping turtles can grow to weigh about 35 pounds (16 kg) and live for about 30 years in the wild.

12

4. Snapping turtles cannot breathe underwater. They have to come up to the surface for air. However, they can hold their breath for a long time.

5. Snapping turtles kill other turtles by using their strong jaws to bite off their heads.

6. Turtles living in places with cold weather **hibernate** during the winter. They bury themselves in mud or sand and do not move or come up for air for 4 or 5 months.

7. Snapping turtles cannot pull their head and legs into their shell, as many other turtles can.

8. Snapping turtles use smell, eyesight, and touch to sense nearby animals. They might also feel vibrations in the water.

Laying Eggs

Snapping turtles generally **mate** between April and June. After mating, the female turtle leaves the water to find a sunny spot to lay her eggs. She makes a nest by digging a hole in sand or soil. Then, she lays between 20 and 50 eggs in the nest. When she is done, she covers the eggs with sand or soil and returns to the water.

These baby snapping turtles are breaking out of their shells. Soon they will crawl to the water.

You can see the dug up earth behind this female snapping turtle. She is laying her eggs in the hole.

After about 100 days, the eggs hatch. The tiny turtles, called hatchlings, are about the size of a quarter. They use their claws and a special tooth to break out of their shells. Then, they crawl out of the nest toward the water.

What Snappers Eat

Snapping turtles are omnivores. That means they eat both plants and animals. They are also scavengers. This means they will eat dead animals that they find. They are not picky eaters.

In the water, snapping turtles may eat insects, fish, clams, crayfish, birds, frogs, worms, snakes, and other turtles. They also eat many different kinds of aquatic plants.

Crayfish are small crustaceans that are related to lobsters. They are eaten by many predators, including snapping turtles.

Common snapping turtles will eat almost anything they can find!

Snapping turtles must eat underwater. They need the **pressure** from the water to be able to swallow their food. Snapping turtles hunt by lying still until their prey swims or floats by. Then, they quickly lunge at their prey and snap their jaws to catch it.

17

Adult snapping turtles have almost no animal predators. Their hard carapaces and powerful jaws keep them safe from attacks by other animals.

However, hatchings are often killed by animal predators. They are much smaller and have softer shells than adults do, which makes them **vulnerable**. Hawks, herons, crows, raccoons, snakes, skunks, foxes, and dogs all eat snapping turtle hatchlings.

Snapping turtle eggs are at risk of being eaten by predators.

Hawks prey on many different animals, including baby snapping turtles.

In the water, hatchlings' predators are alligators, fish, and other turtles. Hatchlings hide from predators among aquatic plants. Animal predators also steal eggs from snapping turtle nests. Turtle nests are not protected because female turtles go back to the water after laying their eggs.

Hatchlings do not have tough shells, as adult snapping turtles do. They hide to keep safe from predators.

19

People and Snappers

Native American peoples have used snapping turtle shells in **ceremonies** for a long time. The shells are sometimes dried and filled with corn kernels to make rattles.

People also hunt snapping turtles for their meat. The meat is used in soups and stews. Turtle hunting is allowed in several states.

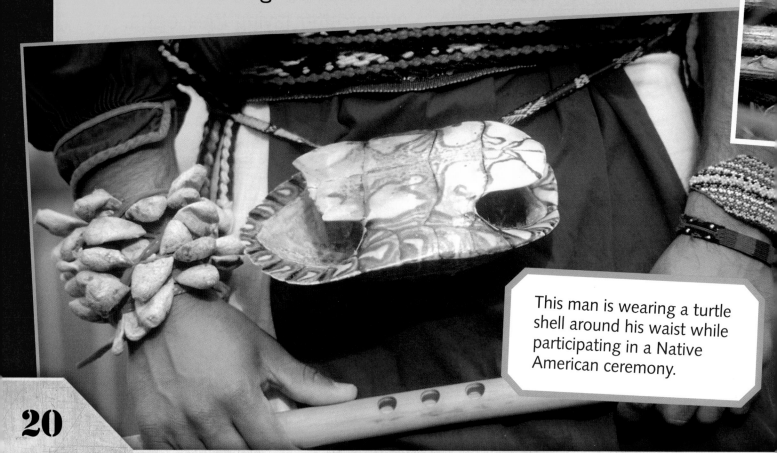

This man is wearing a turtle shell around his waist while participating in a Native American ceremony.

Unlike many other animals, snapping turtles can live in polluted waters. Their exposure to chemicals and pollution can make them unsafe for people to eat.

However, in other states, it is not allowed. Some scientists think people should not eat snapping turtles. This is because their bodies can absorb **chemicals** from pollution that are harmful to people.

Each year, people also accidentally kill snapping turtles. This often happens when a snapping turtle wanders on to a road and is hit by a car.

Snappers Today

Today, snapping turtles are not in danger of dying out. In fact, they are very **adaptable** animals. They can survive even when people pollute their habitats. However, polluted habitats may kill the plants and animals that snapping turtles eat. It is always important to take care of wildlife.

If you see a snapping turtle in the water, it is safe to watch them. However, if you see a snapping turtle on land, you should stay far back. They may lunge and snap at you!

Glossary

adaptable (uh-DAPT-eh-bul) To change to fit new conditions.

aggressive (uh-GREH-siv) Ready to fight.

ceremonies (SER-ih-moh-neez) A special series of actions done on certain occasions.

chemicals (KEH-mih-kulz) Matter that can be mixed with other matter to cause changes or harm.

habitats (HA-buh-tats) The surroundings where an animal or a plant naturally lives.

hibernate (HY-bur-nayt) To spend the winter in a sleeplike state.

mate (MAYT) To come together to make babies.

polluted (puh-LOO-ted) To make air, water, or soil dirty and harmful to living things.

predators (PREH-duh-terz) Animals that kills other animals for food.

pressure (PREH-shur) A force that pushes on something.

range (RAYNJ) The area of land or water where a species of animal might live.

reptiles (REP-tylz) Cold-blooded animals with lungs and scales.

vulnerable (VUL-neh-ruh-bel) Open to attack or harm.

Index

Websites

Due to the changing nature of Internet links, PowerKids Press has developed an online list of websites related to the subject of this book. This site is updated regularly. Please use this link to access the list: www.powerkidslinks.com/aaa/turtl/

24